These affirmations were created during my early morning devotional time over a span of 4 years. I found it to be God's way of reminding me to acknowledge His love for me in the "simple things" in life. Each morning, I was blessed with a Simple Confession of Love that I focused on throughout the day. During the rough moments of my day, I would repeat my Simple Confession like an affirmation in order to get my mind back on track.

There are endless ways that the love of God is simply confessed to us. I hope that each Simple Confession in this book will be used as an affirmation to draw you closer to the Creator and to your "purposed" self.

I have included 2 Simple Confessions per page that can be used as an a.m. and a p.m. affirmation. You can use the a.m. affirmation throughout your day to focus or refocus your mind on the positive throughout the day. You can use the p.m. affirmation as part of your nightly routine to focus your mind as you wind down your day. I pray that your love for the Creator and yourself grows with each Simple Confession you read to affirm your "purposed" self.

Dr. Jacqueline Jones
Simply Loved by God

There is a God who loves you and there is nothing you can do to change that

It's impossible to hide from or escape the love of your Creator.

The God who loves you created you from a perfect model.

The God who loves you is the only standard of measurement worthy of any comparison.

The God who loves you knows
your true value & worth much
better than any other.

The God who loves you is
also the One who is the
most faithful to you.

The God who loves you is the only One who can truly handle your cares that you cast upon Him.

The God who loves you has NO plans of ever giving up on you.

There is a Sovereign God
who loves you, so don't allow it
to matter when others don't

The God who loves you has
no limits or ending time on
His love for you.

The God who loves you
accepted you based on what
He did for you not what you
do for Him.

There is no end to the love
God has for you.

The God who loves you is never idle.

The God who loves you doesn't just offer you solutions; He offers Himself as the Solution.

How many days did you affirm yourself?

_____

How did you feel about affirming yourself?

_____

_____

_____

_____

What is 1 thing you are proud of this week?

_____

_____

The God who loves you
wants you to love the
person He knows you are.

The God who loves you
does so without conditions.

The God who loves you
gives you a choice to make
purpose or make plans.

The God who loves you is
also the Source of your love
for others.

The God of hope loves you
and wants you to prosper
in His will above all things.

The God who loves you is
also committed to the
purpose He created in you.

The God who loves you is also the One most loyal to you.

The width, depth, height nor the length of God's love for you can be measured.

The God who loves you made you to be the "living reality" of His love for people.

The God who loves you rearranges, shifts & adjusts as necessary to keep you on your path of purpose.

The one you waited your whole life for is the God who already loved you.

The God who loves you made you a connecting piece in His Masterpiece.

The God who loves you set you apart. Why do you keep trying to fit in?

Sometimes the God who loves you aligns your victory with the Cross He asked that you bear.

How many days did you affirm yourself?

_____

How did you feel about affirming yourself?

_____

_____

_____

_____

What is 1 thing you are proud of this week?

_____

_____

The God who loves you is
named I Am...
(The next words are your choice.)

The God who loves you wants
you to concern yourself with
serving His people not pleasing
them.

The God who loves you has answers to questions you have yet to ask.

It is not possible for the God who loves you to fail or to fail you.

The God who loves you is not of this world. Now stop being anxious about this world.

The God who loves you is Omnipresent. There is no need to search for Him.

The Sovereign God with all power who loves you gave you an extraordinary power to love.

The God who loves you is more focused on you than your problems.

According to the God who loves you, when you do unto others with joy, you get refreshed.

The God who loves you is also the light in you. Now let your light shine.

There is a God who loves
you and that love has never
been hidden.

The God who crafted you
is the God who loves you.

Let's be in awe of the God
who loves us more for who
He is than what He can do.

There is a God who loves
you which means there is a
Trinity who loves you.

How many days did you affirm yourself?

_____

How did you feel about affirming yourself?

_____

_____

_____

_____

What is 1 thing you are proud of this week?

_____

_____

There is a God who loves you in a reckless manner. This love can destroy all the other mess in your life.

The God who loves you really does
#heartyou
#likeyou
#loveyou
#followyou

The God who loves you
created you so unique that
#comparison is useless.

The light of the God who loves
shines brightly to keep you on
your path of purpose.

The God who loves you is the Creator of the truth you are in search of.

The God who loves you is the best GPS source when you are traveling toward your destiny.

It is difficult to hear the voice of the God who loves you when you are surrounded by the noise of your life.

The God who loves you continues to offer a calming grace that also rescues you.

The God who loves you has a map to walk in His ways. It's called faith

The will of the God who loves you won't always meet your expectations but He will meet your needs.

The God who loves you
doesn't take the weekends
or the holidays off.

The God who loves you isn't
just waiting for your prayers.
He's waiting for you to believe
in them.

The God who loves you
operates by His will not
time.

The God who loves you is the
Living,
Sovereign,
I Am
God.

How many days did you affirm yourself?

_____

How did you feel about affirming yourself?

_____

_____

_____

_____

What is 1 thing you are proud of this week?

_____

_____

The God who loves you is your foundation. It's up to you to keep it watered.

The God who loves you gave you an example so that you could be an example.

The God who loves you sent you a

message

#ReadHisWord

You can find how much He loves you

there.

The God who loves you planted

a seed in you that is watered by

the Spirit and grows at His

command.

The God who loves you created you to love His image in others.

Rather than "facing" tough situations,
you could try "facing" the God who loves you.

The God who loves you has given you all that you need to conquer today.

Go ahead & update your status: In an eternal relationship with the God who is love.

The God who loves you
didn't wait for you to choose
Him. He 1st chose you.

The God who loves you
wants to see you worship
during your waiting.

The God who loves you
sacrificed a lot for you.

The God who loves you gave
you a measure of grace that is
sufficient for anything you
need.

The Sovereign God who loves
you knows His plans for you as
well as the enemy's plans
against you.

The God who loves you
also forgives and restores
you.

How many days did you affirm yourself?

_____

How did you feel about affirming yourself?

_____

_____

_____

_____

What is 1 thing you are proud of this week?

_____

_____

The God who loves you isn't just a good, great or the best part of your life. He is your life because your life is in Him.

The God who loves you and has never forsaken you certainly isn't going to start now.

The God who loves you steps
into the deepest and darkest
areas of your heart and shines
the light of His love.

The God who loves you
provides "truth" to you &
holds you responsible for it

The God who loves you uses
every circumstance & situation
in your life to draw you closer
to Him.

The God who loves you
understands how much your
future generations need you to
love Him.

The God who loves you wants you to

submit

sacrifice

surrender.

The God who loves you wants
you to find your worth and
value completely in Him.

The God who loves you now
and loved you then will
continue to love you later.

Simple Confessions
of Love
©

The God who loves you
will complete "every" good
work He started in you.

The God who loves you is the answer to that question or problem you have been wrestling with lately.

The God who loves you provided you with a bridge of reconciliation to Himself.

The God who loves you
understands you. Yes! even
better than you know yourself.

The God who loves you
just does!

How many days did you affirm yourself?

_____

How did you feel about affirming yourself?

_____

_____

_____

_____

What is 1 thing you are proud of this week?

_____

_____

The God who loves you casts away worry, anxiety & fear. Don't jump ship to reclaim them.

The God who loves you provided you with a great reason to rejoice. Look in the mirror.

The God who loves you from the "inside/out" also blesses you from the "outside/in".

The power, prosperity and provision are found in the presence of the God who loves you.

The God who loves you created you for purpose. No one can ever devalue or decrease that purpose.

The God who loves you increases the impact of your prayers according to His will and your purpose.

The God who loves you has forgiven you more than you can ever forgive others.

The God who loves you is also the light in you.

The God who loves you communicates with you each day through His creation.

Simple Confessions of Love

A small amount of faith in a big God who loves you goes a long way to produce unfathomable results.

The toughest love of the God who loves you is infinitely greater than the greatest love you will find on earth

The God who loves you desires your inner worship over your verbal worship.

The God who loves you calls you into "the deep" because that's where the blessings you are seeking are located.

The God who loves you awaits you faith-centered prayers.

How many days did you affirm yourself?

_____

How did you feel about affirming yourself?

_____

_____

_____

_____

What is 1 thing you are proud of this week?

_____

_____

The God who loves you
didn't wait for you to love
Him 1st

Because the Sovereign God
loves you, there is NO need
to ever give up, lose faith, or
lose hope.

The God who loves you
floods your life with His
promises.

The God who loves you
welcomes you each day
with a new mercy.

There is a God who loves you
and your reverential fear
reveals your faith in Him.

The more you behave like the
God who loves you, the less you
will have to regret behaving like
the person you shouldn't be.

The God who loves you has purposed you with destiny.

The God who loves you shines like a bright light in the darkest places in your life.

The God who loves & lives
in you creates an overflow
of life through you.

The God who loves you
ties your abundant life to
your obedience.

The God who loves you

gives you grace to season

your speech

The God who loves you has it

all figured out

Now you just need to

faith it out

The God who lives in you
also lives among you.

The God who loves you has
already made provisions for every
problem, circumstance, hurt, pain,
suffering, etc. that will happen in
your lifetime.

How many days did you affirm yourself?

_____

How did you feel about affirming yourself?

_____

_____

_____

_____

What is 1 thing you are proud of this week?

_____

_____

The God who loves you
doesn't want your expectancy
to turn into entitlement

Your heart of obedience
should be greater than
your lips of praise.

The God who loves you
gives you the freedom to
live out your faith

The God who loves you has
already supplied your
greatest need.

The God who loves you is Sovereign which eliminates any need to worry.

In order to be like the God who loves you, spend time with Him and you shall be like Him.

The God who loves you is moved by the actions of your faith more than the words you speak

The God who loves you gives you opportunities to express your love for Him in your faith walk.

The God who loves you
planted the seed of His Word
in you.
Don't forget to water it

Your Monday - Saturday
life is as important to God
as your Sunday praise.

The God who loves you never
puts distance between you and
Him.
A lack of faith does that

The God who loves you
also loves the person you
might be refusing to love.

The God who loves you speaks
these words to you:
Do not be afraid.
Take Courage!

There is a God who loves
you & that makes every
day a holiday.

How many days did you affirm yourself?

_____

How did you feel about affirming yourself?

_____

_____

_____

_____

What is 1 thing you are proud of this week?

_____

_____

The God who loves you is the one responsible for the power behind your prayers.

The God who loves you is also the Champion who defends you.

Our EXTRA ordinary God chooses to meet you in the ordinary moments of your life because He loves you in an UN ordinary way.

Simple Confessions of Love

God's love for you is purposed with His power in you.

When you are rooted in the God who loves you, the storms of life are but a nice breeze.

The presence of the God who loves you will always override any circumstance you encounter.

The light of God who lives in you shines brightest in your darkest hour.

The God who loves you will never allow you to be in a position where you cannot feel His love.

The God who loves you offers you rest in His presence.

Simple Confessions of Love

God never grows weary of loving you.

When you choose to worry, you are also choosing to dismiss the Power, Sovereignty, and Favor of the God who loves you.

The favor of the God who loves you is as simple as your next breath, & as complex as the manner in which your body functions.

The God who loves you wants
you to be more than just a giver
of things.

The hype of God's love
for you doesn't begin or
end on a single day.

There is never one second of your life when God is not revealing His love for you.

The God who loves you sometimes allows you to travel a rough road so you can see your true character.

Each morning's sunrise is one of
the myriad of ways God shows
His love for you.

The God who loves you
wrote the end of the story.
Spoiler Alert –
You win!

How many days did you affirm yourself?

_____

How did you feel about affirming yourself?

_____

_____

_____

_____

What is 1 thing you are proud of this week?

_____

_____

CPSIA information can be obtained
at www.ICGtesting.com
Printed in the USA
BVHW051605290421
606136BV00010B/1077